The Me I *Used* to Be...

The Me I *Used* to BE:

Sexual & Physical Trauma
Through the Eyes of a Child
Volume I

Erica Lynn White, LMSW

Publisher: IMPACCTT Enterprises, P.L.L.C

Copyright 2019

Disclaimer: This is a work of nonfiction. Some names and identifying information have been left out to protect the privacy of individuals. I have tried to recreate events, locales, and conversations from my memories of them. I may have changed some identifying characteristics and details. Although the author and publisher have made every effort to ensure that the information in this book is correct, the author and publisher do not assume and hereby disclaim any liability to any party for any loss, damage, or disruption caused by errors or omissions, whether such errors or omissions result from negligence, accident, or any other cause.

Printed in the United States
ISBN: 9781073581672

Writing Coach
Jeri Darby

**Children are a heritage from the Lord,
offspring a reward from Him.**

PSALM 127: v.3

Dedication

This is the story of my journey through the foster care system in the town of Saginaw, Michigan. I entered care at the age of five and aged out of care at the age of eighteen. This story is dedicated to my siblings whom I am extremely proud of and the confident, strong, victorious, beautiful, intelligent, and compassionate woman that I am today.

My siblings and I have come a long way. We survived what some would not have been able to withstand, and we have been fortunate to go from surviving to thriving. To my little brother Johnny, my grandfather Joe Swilley, my birth mother Juanita Swilley, and my spiritual mother Aunt Diane Staples, I hope that this book makes you all smile with pride as you watch over us from above. You all are so loved by me.

To God and my Lord and Savior Jesus Christ, thanks for being everything I could ever ask for. To You be all praises. I offer you all of me.

Table of Content

Introduction

THIS IS THE STORY of my journey through the foster care system in the town of Saginaw, Michigan. I entered care at the age of five and aged out of care at the age of eighteen.

To the reader, I hope that this story inspires you to face life challenges with boldness and courage. We all have the capacity to hurt and to likewise heal. I pray that you will commit to healing in order to experience emotional freedom. We all deserve full lives. There is only one you, and you have to be busy about taking care of you. You have the power to choose health, life, and peace. Don't be afraid to reclaim and redefine your life. It is a gift that you have been given. Embrace it and be enriched by it. Be blessed and BE FREE in Jesus name!!

Prologue

I LOOKED FORWARD to my day in court. I couldn't wait to get on the stand to tell everyone about the evil and vile things Curtis had done to me. Prior to the court date, my foster care worker arranged for me to talk with the judge and to see a layout of the courtroom. They explained where everyone would be seated. I was aware that my grandfather, my foster care worker, and the judge would be there to support me. I was also told that a bailiff would be present to ensure that everyone was safe.

On the morning of the hearing, I remember waking up with a feeling of confidence and strength because I knew that I was supported, loved, and believed! I put on my best dress which was a light pink Easter style dress from Burlington, white tights, and matching pink patent leather shoes with a bow on top. I felt like a beautiful princess in that dress! My grandfather drove me to the hearing. We chatted in the car, and he reassured me that I would be okay. He reminded me that I could look at him if I felt afraid and encouraged me to take my time in telling the truth. He told me to tell *everything* so that Curtis would never have the chance to do what he did to me to anyone else.

I was ready to make him feel as small as he made my siblings and I feel every day that we spent in that house of pain. He would no longer be able to hide behind his fake smile and snakelike charm after I told my truth!

Chapter

Where Did Mommy Go?

MY EARLIEST MEMORIES are somewhat fragmented and marked by events that I now realize that I experienced as traumatic. I recall one incident at the age of four. My siblings and I were huddled and asleep on the floor of the home of my mother's then boyfriend. Her boyfriend was also sleeping on the floor. After everyone was asleep on this particular night, her boyfriend fondled me between my legs. I didn't know what he was doing or why he was doing that, but I sensed it wasn't right, and I didn't like it. I got up and laid down next to my oldest

3

brother. Her boyfriend did not bother me anymore after I did. I always have felt safe around my big brother.

On another day within the same home, I remember feeling confused and scared as my siblings and I witnessed the same boyfriend beating my mother all over her body with a broom in the hallway of the house. I remember my siblings and I being very still and quiet as we watched. We had never seen anything like that before. My mother could do nothing to protect or shield herself from the contact with the wooden broom, but I don't remember her screaming or crying in front of us. The attack seemed to come out of nowhere. I remember feeling so afraid for my mom. As a teenager, I learned more about that boyfriend, and that I was right to have been afraid for my mom. That man was not known as a nice person by many people within the community.

On yet another day, I remember my oldest brother trying to boil hot dogs and then feeding the hotdogs to the rest of us. When the hot dogs were gone, we ate fish bones out of the trash can. The bones smelled bad, but it beat being hungry. On this day, I remember noticing that my mother was gone for a long time. I recall my grandfather coming to check on my siblings and I, and that he looked very sad and angry. I remember hearing people talking about not being able to find my mother. I remember the fear that I felt as my grandfather's blue Cadillac pulled up to the same house followed by the police cars.

My grandfather looked broken-hearted as he and the officers entered our home and packed our bags. After we were loaded in the car with our limited possessions, we were taken to the Saginaw County Child Receiving Home. The Saginaw County Child Receiving Home (previously located on Hospital Road) was converted into another company years ago. It was a well-known temporary emergency shelter for youth transitioning to enter either foster care or the juvenile detention facility.

The staff at the Receiving Home were very nice. I would get to know them very well over the course of my childhood. I transitioned there after every placement disruption. The first time there was scary for my siblings and I. We had never been split up before. My sister and I were in a different room from my two brothers. We had to have our hair washed with weird smelling shampoo. We couldn't wear our own clothes. Our clothes and toys had to remain packed away. The female staff members had to give the girls a bath, and the male staff gave all of the boys their baths. Every bit of our day was scheduled. We got up early for showers and breakfast with all of the other residents, received transportation to and from school, played together as a community, and all went to bed at the same time.

Things were sad and scary there sometimes. At times, kids that my siblings and I had gotten to know or that we otherwise had become comfortable with seeing every day, would leave. Sometimes, they would leave to go back home. On other occasions, we were told that they were going to new families. I felt left out when that happened. I wanted to go home too. Sometimes, new kids would come in with sad faces and bruises on their bodies.

During my first few days and months in the Saginaw County Child Receiving Home and first foster placement, I recall overhearing my grandfather and case managers having discussions about my Mom. I remember wondering where she was, and when she was going to come to get my siblings and me. I remember sitting in the court room for what I now understand to have been review hearings. I remember that my Mom never showed for those hearings. I had so much hope. I would sit in the quiet of the courtroom with my siblings, grandfather, case manager, and the judge. I would stare at the door waiting for my Mom. I just knew that she loved us, and that she was going to "come and get us."

I remember the silence on the car rides back from the court. I remember missing my Mom as much as a five-year-old could. I remember hoping that she would show up to prove everyone wrong. I was hoping that she would prove that she loved us by coming back for us and telling the court why she had been gone. She never came.

At the age of five, I didn't have the words or the intellect to comprehend, that I didn't simply miss her. I was confused, sad, and mad. I felt alone and rejected. The months came and went, but my Mom continued to miss the hearings. I now understand that the hearings were conducted every ninety days. I recall my grandfather being angry, hurt, and terribly saddened by my mother's lack of response to the court. I remember a phone conversation where it was clear that she was on the other end, and he was telling her that, "The people are going to take your kids if you don't get off that stuff!" At the time, I didn't know who the *people* were or what the *stuff* was. I now understand that *"the people"* represented the State of Michigan Child Protection Services Division and Family Court. Years later, I discovered that *"the stuff"* she was on was heroine. I also learned that my mother committed neglect via leaving us home alone for three days while she was out binging on heroine.

I vaguely recall all of the details of the day when my grandfather pulled up into the driveway of that first foster care placement to pick my siblings and I up for a weekend visit. I always looked forward to my visits with my grandfather. His home on Twelfth Street was a great comfort to my siblings and I. He was a consistent, strong, nurturing, and comforting presence. He was my bridge to my family, my history, and my backbone. He was the glue that held everyone together. Whenever he came pulling up in the Cadillac, my siblings and I knew that love and familiarity would be greeting us. Granddad would usually greet us by saying "Ahhhh Yeah," and smiling that gentle smile that for me seemed to express that all would be well. My grandfather's smile was not present for a while after we were placed in the first home with the Crim's.

As I previously indicated, the weekends were always fun and full of family and love. Granddad had a routine of taking us to the store to get chips and pop. We could also get ice cream off the ice cream truck. My uncles and aunt would come over often, my mother would come over sometimes, and one of my male first cousins was always around as they lived with my grandparents during their teen years. Summers were especially fun because we could walk to the freeze cup house around the corner with my older cousins. We used to have so much fun picking and eating apples off the apple tree in my grandparent's backyard. One of my absolute favorite things to do and one of my best memories was of my grandfather playing his blues records, and dancing with me as I stood on his feet to have some height. We would laugh as we danced around the living room. We would have such a great time!

One weekend was different. My grandfather was different this weekend. He looked tired. This weekend, my grandfather told my siblings and I that my mother would not be able to "get us back." He also told us that "the people were not going to let us live with he and my grandmother because they were too old, and due to their health issues." I'll never forget the look of defeat and weariness upon my grandfather's face that day. Joe Nathion Swilley was as solid a man as they came. He had a poker face unlike any other. That day, my siblings and I felt and shared my grandfather's broken heart. I remember feeling that something terrible had happened.

At the age of five, you can imagine that I didn't really understand what it meant that "my Mom could not get us back." However, I felt the impact and the consequences of her absence long before I had the words to express how I felt. Life was somewhat bearable because my siblings and I were together in our first foster home, and we had weekend visits with my grandfather and family to look forward to. It didn't take long for life to take a terrible turn for me.

I was five when we entered our first placement. This first foster care placement was comprised of a married older couple by the name of Sam and Fannie Crim. The Crim's were quite old when we were placed with them. They lived in a modest, tidy, and neat home on Holland Avenue. (The home was demolished some years ago). They looked and for the most part acted as if they were our substitute grandparents. We were kept clean, fed well, and dressed decently. We were taken to church every Sunday, and Mr. Crim was a Deacon in the church.

Mr. Crim had a terrible secret. He was a child molester. Mr. Crim was the first man to violate my body. Mr. Crim would have sex with me in his marital bed when Mrs. Crim left for church functions, and while my siblings were sleeping. I didn't understand what he was doing. I just knew that it hurt and made me feel dirty, sad, and afraid. I remember wondering what and why he was doing that to me. Little did I know that I would ask this question on numerous occasions in the coming years.

We were in the first placement for three years. I never told anyone what happened. We left that home when an adoptive placement was located for us. I was so relieved to leave. I never told anyone except my Aunt Diane (rest in heaven) what Mr. Crim had done until after he passed away. I suppose that I was demonstrating compassion for what I knew to be a troubled soul by not revealing his secret while he was alive.

Chapter

$$\boxed{2}$$

All That Glitters Is *Not* Gold

As I PREVIOUSLY STATED, we were fortunate to have been identified for a pre-adoptive placement after three years with the Crim's. I was about eight years old at the time, and I felt that I was escaping a level of Hell when we left the Crim's home. We were placed in the home of a married couple by the name of Curtis and Jacquetta Jemerison. Curtis worked in the plant full-time while Jacquetta was a stay at home parent. They didn't have any children of their own at the time of our placement with them.

In the beginning everything seemed fine. My body was not being violated. We were able to eat consistently and well. We were in a nice clean home. We had nice bedrooms. The boys and girls shared rooms with nice new bunk beds. We had decent clothes. The Jemerison's seemed very nice on the surface. They began to talk to my siblings and I about adoption after a month or two within their home. We were excited and felt very fortunate to imagine having a forever family. I recall things going well during the six-month pre-adoptive phase. The date of our formal court adoption proceeding could not come soon enough. I can even recall the adoption day outfits and photo my siblings and I took with the Jemerison's. I remember the huge smiles that we all had in that photo. Little did I know that the photo captured the calm before the storm.

Shortly after the adoption process was completed, things gradually changed for the worse. Curtis started to molest me on a nearly nightly basis once the adoption was finalized. It started out with him pretending to accidentally burst into the bathroom while I was bathing. It quickly escalated. He would wait until everyone was asleep to sneak into my room, get me out of my bed, and take me to another part of the house so that he could have his way with me. When I say molestation, I am speaking of full vaginal penetration and every other imaginable act typically engaged in between two consenting adults was being forced upon me by this nearly six-foot-tall man who was supposed to be a father to me. Curtis would reward me by not beating me as bad as my siblings.

He always told me that he would go easier on my siblings if I kept the sexual molestation a secret and allowed him to perform whatever vile act he desired. On one occasion, I am certain that Jacquetta caught him molesting me. She got up looking for him one night and discovered him on top of me on the floor of the bedroom that I shared with my younger sister. She looked nervous and her eyes were wide as she asked, "What are you doing!" Curtis jumped off of me, hurriedly zipped his pants, and attempted to explain to her that he was trying to help me sleep by warming me up. They both went off to bed and she seemed to accept his explanation. That man disgusted me. *How could she not know the truth!* Denial is a strong defense to the truth.

As I previously indicated, Curtis would physically abuse my siblings and I as well. He would whip us with sticks (switches) and belts which frequently left bruises and welts all over our bodies. On one occasion he beat me with an iron cord. This resulted in me obtaining a terrible scar on my hand which my third-grade teacher noticed and reported to Child Protective Services. Child Protective Services investigated, but they made the mistake of interviewing my siblings and I while the Jemerison's were present in the home. My siblings and I denied everything out of fear that things would get worse if we told.

I have always felt that my brothers got the worst of the physical abuse. My oldest brother received many physical beatings on our behalf as he would take the blame for things in order to try to spare us. Curtis would punch my brothers as if they were grown men out in the street at times, and he seemed to take pleasure in it. He also took pleasure out of mocking their intelligence by pitting the girls against the boys in weird math and reading tests. His wife Jacquetta would destroy property within the home while Curtis was at work, and falsely accuse my siblings and I of doing the damage because she enjoyed the drama of seeing Curtis put us in a circle, interrogate and instill fear within us, and beat us one by one. She would also eat things that they had forbidden us to touch in the refrigerator and accuse us of eating it when he returned home. He would make us all stand in the corner with one of our legs up for hours. If our legs dropped from weariness, he and Jacquetta would take turns striking us with the belt or switch. At times, I would catch her smirking with satisfaction as he tormented us. She was a different kind of dysfunctional.

After about three years of torture with the Jemerison's, we had finally built up the courage to run away. One warm summer day, when neither Curtis nor Jacquetta were looking, my oldest brother led us out the back door of the house of Hades on Janes Street (it has long been torn down). All four of us ran as fast as our feet could carry us to our grandfather's home on 12th street. I'll never forget the freedom of running from that place of torture, or the

14

simultaneous fear that Curtis might find us and beat us before we found our grandfather's home. We were met by my grandfather, my uncle, and one of my first cousins. We told them about the physical abuse that had been happening, and they contacted Child Protective Services.

We were once more placed within the Saginaw County Child Receiving Home. However, we felt more in control on this second time in because "we were standing up for ourselves". The Receiving Home staff and setting was comfortable and scary to us at this time. Comforting because we knew that we were safe. Scary because my siblings and I had come to understand that being within its walls meant that your family was changing for the worst or for the best.

Once we were in the Child Receiving Home and the Child Protection Investigation was completed, we were informed that we could choose to return to the Jemerison's home. Apparently, the Jemerison's had committed to ending their physical disciplinary measures and were making assurances to the authorities that things would be better. My siblings decided to return to the Jemerison's as they were the devils that they *knew* and because they would still be together. I decided that I did not want to return. I hadn't yet shared that Curtis had sexually molested me. I think that I felt that I was protecting my siblings housing option at the time. I didn't want them to be separated from one another.

I was placed in a new foster home with an older teenage girl and several very young foster sisters and brothers while my siblings returned home to the Jemerison's. My home placement was okay in the sense that I was physically safe, had food to eat, had supervision, and had decent clothes to wear. I even had the added bonus of having met my first love while at her home. His family lived just a few houses away. Unfortunately, the foster mother had an open secret. She had a major anger problem and disciplined the kids severely and violently at times. When she became frustrated with some of the young boys' behaviors, she would hit them with belts, pots, pans, and shoes. Sometimes, she would throw whatever she could find at them. I mean anything that she could get her hands on. She always had a home full of children, and she seemed to genuinely love the kids as she ultimately adopted them.

As an older child in the home, I used to worry about them. After all, they were me at certain recent points of my life. My older foster sister and I were conflicted about speaking up to the authorities because we didn't want to have to move again. This foster mother had positive aspects too. She was very loving and generous sometimes. For the most part, she treated me like family, and I really loved her. I loved her family and her family appeared to be really accepting of me. I remember her throwing me my *first* birthday party at the age of seventeen (some years later during the time of my second placement within her home). It was a beautiful party. All of my friends, my boyfriend, foster siblings, her family, and my grandfather were there. It was a beautiful memory!

After some months went by with no visitation with my siblings, I decided to try an overnight visit with them at the Jemerison's home. My siblings had been telling me via phone that things were better, that they weren't being beaten, and that they had new clothes and toys. However, they didn't know that I was hesitant to visit because I didn't want to be molested again.

After a while, I took a chance and decided to visit with my siblings on an overnight weekend visit. On the first overnight of my first visit with my siblings, Curtis once again tiptoed into my room after everyone was asleep. For the first time I allowed myself to feel angry. How dare he try that with me again!! How dare he pretend to be anything different with my siblings! He was a snake! He hadn't changed at all. This time I had the courage to say *"NO!"* and the ability to leave the next day. On the next morning, I told my oldest brother about the molestation and I let him know that I would be telling Child Protective Services about it. He and I discussed fears that Curtis could try to molest my sister if they were to remain there. My brother gave me his full support then as he always has. After I left that day, I called my grandfather and Curtis's sister to tell them my long-held secret. They both told me to speak up and to have courage in doing so.

I'll never forget the day that I told my caseworker about the sexual abuse. I felt as if the weight of the world had been lifted off my then twelve-year-old shoulders. The complaint was investigated and substantiated over the course of a month or two. I had my day in court where I was able to get on the stand and confront my abuser. I remember feeling as strong, defiant, and powerful as any twelve-year-old could on that day. In that courtroom, Curtis did not appear so large physically, in charge, or powerful. Curtis, the offender, seemed small in stature and humble.

For the first time, I realized that he no longer intimidated me emotionally or physically as he sat still and silent at the defense table. My grandfather, my uncles, and my DHS representatives were present. I felt so empowered when a guilty verdict was issued as to all counts of Criminal Sexual Conduct with a minor. Curtis received 25-35 years in prison for what he did to me. I was so proud of myself. I was also relieved that he would *never* again hurt my siblings or anyone else. My voice was being heard...I was safe! I was believed! I was protected! I was cared about! I was a powerful twelve-year-old in that space and time. For the first time since I entered care at the age of five, *I felt in control of myself and my body.*

I should note that Curtis served twenty five of the thirty years that he was sentenced too. Over the years, I occasionally wondered what it would be like if either my siblings or I encountered him within the community. We never had to. Curtis was weak and frail when he was released. He spent his final years on earth in a VA hospital and succumbed to a lengthy illness many years ago. I remember the day I looked for information pertaining to him online and discovered his obituary during my twenties. I called my older brother to inform him. We both fell silent. This was the relief that we needed. This was the *period* on the end of that aspect of our life story.

Erica Lynn White

Chapter

$$\boxed{3}$$

The Bridge

AFTER THE COURT HEARING, one of my great aunt's (my grandfather's sister), made a valiant effort of trying to adopt my siblings and I. I won't speak for the rest of my siblings, but it did not work for me for a couple of reasons. I was too angry to fully receive love. I couldn't believe that my birth family could love me enough to adopt me. In retrospect, I didn't believe that any adult could love me without some type of ulterior motive at that time. It wasn't just mistrust though. I've never told anyone this before, but I realize that I had a valid reason for being angry at my aunt.

My aunt lived with a long-term boyfriend. On one night in particular, she asked me to put on a different gown. In the presence of my youngest sister and her boyfriend, she told me that my choice in my gown showed her that I caused my own sexual abuse. She considered me as *flaunting myself*. I didn't even know what flaunting myself meant. I definitely didn't have any sexual feelings or attractions towards her boyfriend.

Her words hurt in a way that I could not describe at that point in my development. I told myself that I would push the sting of that statement some place deep down inside of me, but I'm pretty sure that I resented her for that. I loved my aunt, but my heart and mind categorized her as an enemy at that time. At that time in my life, people were either good or bad. There was no middle ground. I became even more embittered and assured of my beliefs that adults could not be trusted. I wanted to get as far away from my aunt and her judgments as I could. I purposefully did things to anger her so that she would request that I be moved. I was successful with getting out of the presence of an invalidating and emotionally harmful adult in my eyes.

I know that she was a good person, but I didn't understand where that belief came from. I was her flesh and blood. I was only a *child*. The hardest part about moving was missing my sister and brothers. My brothers had demonstrated behaviors which resulted in their removal and replacement into another foster home together a while before I was relocated. Thankfully, we all had sibling visitation on a consistent basis.

To be impartial about this, I think that there was a general and generational misunderstanding of incest and molestation amongst some of the elders in my family. One of my great uncles, (my great aunt's and my grandfather Joe Swilley's brother) also told me on another occasion during my teen years that he felt that I invited the sexual abuse. His words to me were "It's hard for a man to rape a woman." What I wanted to say but held out of respect for him as my elder, was the fact that I was *not* a woman! Their statements felt as if I was being abused all over again. After I purposefully disrupted my placement within my aunt's home, I was placed within the home of a dear woman who would forever change the course of my life. I was placed with a foster parent by the name of Diane Staples (hereinafter referred to as Aunt Diane).

There is a theory in social work known as attachment theory. Per John Bowlby (well- known attachment theorist, clinician, and author), 1)the quality of the child's relationship with a nurturing parent/ caregiver from the ages of zero to five, and 2)the child's environment are important factors towards: Determining whether the child develops healthy worldviews; a positive self-image; healthy beliefs; a sense of safety/security; and confidence towards achieving developmental tasks necessary to mature into a healthy and productive adult (A Secure Base: Parent- Child Attachment and Healthy Human Development, 1988).

I experienced this life changing relationship during my teen years. Diane was that one positive parent connection that served as my permanent model of love, acceptance, healthy values, and what a healthy parent/child relationship should look like. Aunt Diane transitioned into her heavenly home in July 2014. For me, she was the mother that I never had, but always needed and wanted. It was very hard for me to admit and see it back then. She was a happy, healthy, generous, and vibrant being. She loved me in the midst of and through my hurt, anger, and rebellion. Her home environment was calming and peaceful. She had this way of letting me know that she *saw* me in spite of my wounded heart and discouraged spirit.

Aunt Diane cared about all things concerning me, and she treated me as if I were her daughter as opposed to a foster child. She was the first adult woman with whom I could be 100% of myself. With her, I was consistently emotionally and physically safe. We laughed and cried together. She invested in me. Her biological family was my family. She made sure that I maintained healthy connections with my birth family and advocated for all my needs. Holidays were special, we went to church every Sunday, and she and her friends prayed for me on a consistent basis.

Diane was the first person to gift me with a Christmas ornament with my name engraved on it. I can't explain what it meant to me and how I felt when I first saw it and hung it on the Christmas tree. She took me out for my first birthday dinner and celebration. She ensured that I had a fabulous 9th grade Homecoming Dance experience. There were so many great memories! It was great to just be a kid with no worries or fears about tomorrow. Things were normal. We had normal conversations about relationships, girl talk, and she nurtured my college plans and life goals. She wanted to adopt me, but I couldn't trust *that* level of love at the ripe old age of fourteen. She understood, didn't push me, and continued to love me.

I ultimately ended up accepting Christ as my Savior during my time within Diane's home. I will forever be grateful to her for introducing me to Christ. She also introduced me to the person that I was before all of the pain. She helped me to understand and develop a beginning sense of self. She introduced me to a positive self-image and self-confidence. She directed me towards an understanding that there could be a pathway of healing from my pain and using my experiences for the good. Although it took me many years to fully benefit from everything that she deposited in and modeled for me, I'm so Godly grateful that she took the time.

Erica Lynn White

Chapter

The Broken Pathway

I ULTIMATELY SABOTAGED this home after a nearly three-year placement. I can state with certainty that if it were not for having known the love and consistency of Diane Staples, I would not be here or the woman I am today. Although, I left her home, we never left one another's lives. I'll return to more of this discussion later. I knew that it broke Diane's and my own heart when the placement disrupted. I ended up back at the Child Receiving Home. When she dropped me off, I tried to pretend that I was happy with my victory of seemingly pushing her away.

She knew better, and she quietly wept for me during the car ride over, as she dropped me off, and as she drove away. On one hand, I had actually tried to convince myself that I was happy to be free of a love which I was convinced would go bad eventually. On the other hand, I knew that I had really hurt myself and the first woman that really and consistently demonstrated love for me. My thinking was distorted as I didn't realize then that I had sabotaged myself. You see up until that time, every experience with adults with the exception of my experiences with Diane and my grandfather had taught me that adults in general were unreliable, untrustworthy, manipulative, and abusive. I had learned to live my life with the mindset that things were going to go wrong even if it took a while for it to do so. I allowed my beliefs to influence my behaviors, and the result was a self-fulfilling prophecy with respect to the placement with Diane.

The Receiving Home staff welcomed me back. When they asked me what happened, I was too ashamed to say. I put up a façade of being okay. Aunt Diane was so much of a lady that she didn't tell them either. She always shielded me. I missed her as soon as she drove off. I had never cried about a disrupted placement. However, I cried myself to sleep that night, and many nights thereafter. Oh yes, I cried a river. I immediately missed the love, safety, acceptance, comfort, and peace of her home and presence. I continued my migration into and through three homes thereafter. I was sixteen by the time I entered my sixth placement. To put things nicely, this placement was next level weird. The foster mother was a single elderly woman. This lady rarely left her room or the home, so I thought of her as the hermit lady. The home was small and very unkempt. I mean every room in the home was very dusty and cluttered all of the time. It reminded me of one of the old scary homes from the black and white movie era. It also smelled horribly of cat food and cat urine.

The worst aspect of the home was that I experienced being treated as a foster child; an *"other"* as opposed to a member of the family for the first time in a very clear way. There was another foster child there, but we weren't allowed to talk to one another much. We couldn't watch television. Meals consisted of one serving only and very small portions regardless to what was being served. Servings were measured out.

For example, we received one bowl of cereal or oatmeal consisting of two actual measuring cups of cereal or oatmeal. If we were still hungry, we could not receive more. I often went to school with hunger pains. If that wasn't bad enough, she would fix our cereal and pour the milk on it or cook the oatmeal and set it out well before we were awake or otherwise ready for breakfast. Subsequently, our cereal was soggy, or the oatmeal was cold. It was either eat gross food or go hungry.

During the weeknights and weekends, the cabinets and refrigerators were padlocked after my foster sibling and I were served. We did not have snacks. With respect to our very small meals, my foster sibling and I often went to bed hungry and we were starving by the next morning. Hermit lady didn't treat her grandchildren like she treated us. When they came over, they had access to the food in the fridge and the cabinets as the padlocks were removed. They were also able to ask for seconds.

My time in this home was very brief. I ran away after about a month or so. I couldn't take the depressing and oppressive environment. On the day that I ran away, I chose to stop running when I arrived at my grandfather's home. He listened to and empathized with me, but he encouraged me to stay put due to concerns for my safety if I were to leave his home at that time of night. He had no choice other than to alert my Foster Care Worker. I was transported to the Receiving Home by my foster care worker the next morning. Unlike other times, I welcomed the return to the shelter this time.

At least I was accepted in there, had kids and adults I could talk to, was fed well, and never went to bed hungry. I remember having a longer than usual stay of about a few months due to having been labelled as a runaway. My foster care worker let me know that the runaway behaviors made it more difficult for potential foster parents to decide to take me in. I remember wondering if those same foster parents were ever informed, or otherwise considered just what it was that I was running away from.

I was excited once the new placement was relocated. It had been a long few months in the Receiving Home. I was informed that I would be moving in with a middle-aged single woman who was newly licensed as a foster parent.

Upon meeting the new foster mother, she seemed quite friendly. She also seemed to be mildly out of it. I noticed right away that she looked sad most of the time, stuttered a lot, had a persistent facial tic, seemed really eager to please me, was a bit off balance when she walked, and that her hands shook a lot. She also seemed to struggle with maintaining eye contact during conversation. She often looked down at the ground or off to the side when I or other people would conversate directly with her.

The new foster home was decent in terms of cleanliness and size, but it was nearly barren of furniture and decorative items with the exceptions of basic furniture items. The living room contained a television and an old and tattered sectional sofa. The kitchen was small with no room for a table and chairs. There were three bedrooms. The foster mother had her own room which she kept locked. There were bunk beds and dressers in the other two rooms. I was the first foster child there, so I had my choice of bedrooms and bunk placement.

However, the foster parent informed me that more teenage foster youth would be coming soon. I was relieved when I saw that the refrigerator was fully stocked and that she didn't have a padlock on it or any of the kitchen cabinets. I also noticed that she kept a pretty good stock of 40-ounce Colt 45 beers around. To be frank, it appeared as if the foster parent was barely getting by financially. I soon discovered that she worked a full-time job at minimum wage in a bread bakery. She was no role model and she demonstrated a great deal of questionable conduct and judgment during my time there.

For example, there were times when she would walk around drinking out of the big 40-ounce beer bottles to the point of drunkenness while I was present in the home. She would take the drink into her room at times, but she would emerge stumbling and smelling like beer. I soon learned that she was dating or simply hooking up and having sex with married men for money. There were many times when I overheard her sexually charged phone conversations discussing plans to get together, have sex, and have the men give "her some money to hold." Those different men would often come to the home during the evening while I was there to be met by her walking around in seductive barely there clothing, offering them drinks, and taking them into her bedroom. I knew that they were having sex because I could hear the bed squeaking. They would emerge later during the night or early on the next morning with the foster mother coming out with tousled hair, clothing, and smelling like alcohol and sex. They would head straight into the shower. She really never seemed to give any thought to the fact that I was seeing all of that.

It didn't take long for me to understand that I could do and actually began doing whatever I wanted. To be fair, I'm not blaming the foster mother. Her home environment was simply the opportunity for me to begin to act out. At the age of sixteen, the sexual and physical abuse and my negative experiences within care had left me with plenty of my own faulty thinking, beliefs, and damaged emotions. I ran with a rough crowd for a time, experimented with drinking, smoking weed, and partied a lot in an effort to mask my pain and sadness. I looked for acceptance and love in the wrong places and with the wrong type of guys. I compromised the sanctity of my body with guys because I had associated sex with affection and love.

As a teenager, it took a while to figure out that I was hurting myself with my behaviors. My come to Jesus moment was when the foster mother told me that she heard my name was "ringing in the streets." I imagine that she was right. She told me this a few nights after I had gotten so drunk that I couldn't move or talk. On the night in particular, an adult neighborhood guy took full advantage of my nearly comatose state. I was terribly ashamed about that night. I didn't report the incident because I felt that I was to blame because I had been drinking. I also didn't want to experience rejection or retaliation by him, or isolation within my then peer group.

I now understand that it was rape by way of my inability to consent via my age and state of inebriation. I felt shame course through my being for a moment after she said that. In that moment, I defiantly thought to myself that I could say the same if not worse about her. Prior to that night, I was running the streets at all times of day and night, coming home plastered, and doing other things right up under her nose. She never called me out on any of it. She never said a word as she was happy to let me do whatever I wanted so long as she kept cashing her foster care stipend checks. I and the other girls were her meal tickets. The lack of rules, boundaries, and expectations worked for me until I realized that I had become ashamed and embarrassed by my own behavior. I didn't respect her, and I couldn't talk to her as she seemed to be struggling with low self-esteem, loneliness, financial stress, and alcoholism. In my eyes, she was another adult hypocrite who didn't care about me; but wanted to benefit from me. I felt that I was at an all-time low with regard to my conduct and confidence within her home.

I hated to admit it, but my freedom wasn't free in that home. It cost me a lot in terms of my pride and ego. I missed the structure, routine, and morals of Aunt Diane's home. I felt that there was no returning there though. Even though Aunt Diane and I had maintained phone contact across time, I felt there was no going back. The tipping point came quickly as soon thereafter the foster mother filled the three other beds with several wilder teens. It became a very overwhelming environment for me. I ran away to my grandfather's house again. However, I was running away from the home and the person that I became and began to hate in that environment.

Chapter

5

The Return Home

AFTER I RAN AWAY, I only had to go to the Receiving Home for a week or so. Someone had informed me that the foster mother that I lived with during my first individual placement had an opening. I informed my foster care worker of this and I was able to return to the home. By this time, I was sixteen and a half years old, and midway through my tenth-grade year in high school. I had to switch school districts, but I was able to adjust well. I made friends quickly, and I had always done well academically due to school having been an escape from the chaos of my life during my early childhood. The home was different in that the little kids were older, and my former older teenage foster sister was no longer there. I was the only teen there this time. I resumed my relationships with her family members, and my childhood sweetheart who still lived a few homes away.

The home environment was calmer and happier this time around. There wasn't as much frustration and angst evident in the foster mother or the children (most of whom she had adopted by this time). The foster mother seemed calmer. She did not hit the children as much at this time. The foster mother and my grandfather eventually started and maintained a long-term relationship with each other. This was a bonus for me as I loved every opportunity I had with him. They seemed happy and content with each other. That made me happy, and made the placement feel even more like a home and family to me.

During this time, I experienced my first birthday party (17th b-day) complete with a taco dinner (one of my favorite foods by the way), a cake, ice cream, friends, family, music, laughs, and love courtesy of my foster mother. It was and is one of the best memories of my lifetime! That really meant a lot to me. It was great for things to be *normal* for a change. It was wonderful to be celebrated and acknowledged in that way.As I indicated, the placement was good. I was in a different and better place both emotionally and physically. I was no longer drinking, partying, running the streets with a rough crowd, or looking for love. I felt supported, accepted, and loved within my home, school and relationships. I completed my tenth-grade year without incident. I entered the eleventh grade in good standing. I fell behind a bit due to too much socializing for a time, but I was able to pull myself out of the academic slump by attending summer school over that summer. By the time of my twelfth-grade year, I had renewed my commitment to Christ, and I was attempting to engage in a deeper walk with Him.

That caused some friction between my boyfriend and I and resulted in the end of the relationship for that period of our lives. Otherwise, things continued to go well up through to the time of a house fire which resulted in a great deal of smoke damage to the inside of the home, and the loss of all of our belongings close to the end of my senior year. I could care less about the belongings as I was glad to be alive. I escaped that fire with nothing but my undergarments on. We managed to relocate and adjust to a temporary rental home while the other home was remodeled. My church supported us in ensuring that I had a great prom experience. It really was phenomenal!

In the months leading up to prom and graduation, the conversation gradually shifted to the subject of emancipation. Everyone is aware that the age of being a legal adult is eighteen. For a youth in foster care, eighteen is the age at which the state is no longer legally responsible for you. This can be further interpreted as the foster parent will no longer receive payments for services or resources towards the foster child's care. I had definitely been thinking of my next steps, and my foster mom and I talked about it often. I knew that I needed and wanted to work.

I desired to attend community college in order to pursue a degree in social services, and I wanted to have my own apartment. I finally reached out to my foster care worker for options in the aftermath of being appalled and outraged that my foster mother suggested that I "get pregnant so that I can get on welfare and have a source of income in order to afford my own apartment." I'm still uncertain as to whether that was her worldview (an idea of how to get to get ahead in life), her perceptions of my potential in my life—or both. I ended up not having to worry about resources thanks to my long-term foster care worker, Patti Jo Bolyard.

Mrs. Bolyard (as she was known then) prepped me for post-graduation a great deal by providing me with information about a program in place at the time called the Independent Living Program for Foster Care Youth. At the time, this particular program provided the following: 1) a rental deposit and rent payments; 2) two years of case management support; 3) assistance with establishing utilities; 4) initial purchase of household furniture and goods; 5) guidance in establishing and maintaining checking and savings accounts; and 6) support in purchase of initial books and other school supplies during the first four years of college for emancipated foster care youth who graduated high school.

I was empowered towards completing my senior year with knowledge that I would be supported and allowed to transition out of care. I was fortunate as I'm not certain that resources of that scope and nature are still available to emancipated foster care youth in Michigan. My graduation from Saginaw High School was wonderfully joy-filled and carefree. All of these years later, it is still a wonderful memory. With my foster care workers and grandfather's support, and the resources of the Independent Living Program, I moved into my first apartment two weeks after graduation. I felt so proud of my eighteen-year-old self. I obtained my first full time job at Meijer soon thereafter. I also enrolled for classes within the Arts and Sciences Department at Delta College. During my time within placement with Aunt Diane, I was able to identify a desire to help children and families to heal from situations such as what my siblings and I endured in a capacity as either a Psychologist or Social Worker. I was eager to begin work and classes, and I enthusiastically set about my new daily routines of balancing work, a social life, and being a student. It felt wonderful!

There was a larger milestone during this first year on my own. My mother called me one day to inform me that she was no longer on drugs and that she had "gotten saved" and joined a church. I remember feeling as if I was holding my breath when I picked up the phone and heard her voice on the other end. It honestly felt like time slowed down when I talked with her. I can't remember what I said in response, but I recall feeling as if I was overwhelmed with emotion to the extent that I didn't quite know what to say. This particular call communicated a great deal to me. I always had mixed feelings about my mother. I loved her and needed her, but I simultaneously felt anger towards her and hurt by her absence in our lives. I believe that the call was my mother's effort to: 1) admit her faults,; 2) acknowledge my importance to her; 3) let me know that my opinion of her mattered; and 4) provide me with validation of my concerns, and a measure of peace regarding her status in life and my place in her heart. I appreciated her efforts. That day marked the first time that I heard and understood her as clearly attempting to express remorse for not being able to function as my mother. I needed that. I felt a slight softening in the areas of my heart that had attempted to harden towards her. Up until that phone call on that day, I had perceived my mother giving us up as the greatest rejection and loss of my lifetime.

My mother also informed me that my father was dying during that phone call and encouraged me to seek Social Security Survivor's Benefits in the event of his death. I informed her that I didn't want to do that. I preferred to go without that resource. I didn't and still don't have any negative feelings towards my dad. I know his name, and I have a few positive memories of him from my childhood. I remember him seemingly being a happy man that used to take me out for chips and soda at times, cook for me at times, and advocating for me to be able to be allowed to do as I wished. I sensed that he loved me. I also remember that he drove a truck. I went to see him and made peace with him shortly before he died. I remember not having much feeling about his passing because I didn't really know him.

I must share that I would see my mother on various occasions throughout my childhood. There were times that she would pop in while I was visiting with either my grandfather or my aunt (her sister). However, I could not and dared not say anything to any of my foster parents because I wasn't supposed to have any contact with her before or after her parental rights were terminated per the orders of the state. I remember it feeling both comforting, angering, unsettling, and good to see her and be in her presence. As a child, I loved those fleeting moments around her. She would comb our hair and cook for us at times. The touch of my mother's hands was soothing and nurturing, and wow could she cook! I loved when she cooked tacos or fried chicken with greens, okra, and cornbread. It felt so natural with her, and I knew that it would be so easy to forgive her and love her again if I could ever return to live with her.

On the other hand, I would be angry inside because I knew that it would never happen, and that her addiction was to blame. At times, she would stay for a while, but she would never stay around long, or look directly at or talk to my siblings and I much beyond small talk or her occasional nervous laughter. I now understand that she carried a lot of guilt, sadness, and shame for having given us up.

Thus, what appeared as if she was avoiding us was actually her attempting to cope with what I'm sure was the greatest pain of her lifetime. It took me many years to process and understand, but I can honestly say that I respect her and her decision. To say that it couldn't have been easy to do what she did would be an understatement, and though I had my share of trauma with her and within some of the foster care placements, I realize that my life could have gone in a totally different direction if she had not have made the hard and responsible decision to give us what she perceived as opportunities for stability and care that she could not and did not know how to provide.

At the end of the first year on my own, my grandfather made his transition into Heaven. It happened so suddenly from my perspective. Perhaps, it was just that I was protected from knowing the extent of his ongoing health troubles at that time. I can honestly say that I don't know how I endured that. I loved my grandfather so much, and oh how he loved me. I never had to wonder about my place in his heart. It was always a priority during my eighteen years of knowing him. I'll never forget a part of my last conversation with him during which he told me that he had accepted that it may have been time for him to "go home" wherein he said that he was "okay with that because he knew that I was going to be alright." I couldn't imagine life without him, and I didn't want to see him go. However, he was right. I am better than alright!

Chapter

6

The Silver Lining

I CONTINUED ON IN MY STUDIES. I was blessed with great academic performance, and a steady job at Meijer's. I maintained a good work and life balance. I wasn't able to finish the Associate in Arts program in two years at Delta. Subsequently, I faced a dilemma of sorts in that the Independent Living Program cash supports was drawing close to ending as per the two-year timeframe. I had come to realize that it was going to be difficult to maintain an apartment and focus on my academics in the absence of that additional income. Although I was employed, the subsidy helped me to afford the balance of my costs of living. I had to come up with a plan.

As I previously indicated, Diane and I had maintained communication throughout the years. We were in frequent communication after I graduated high school and got out on my own. We would talk over the phone and I would visit with her often. It was very comforting to have her in my life again. We picked up with one another as if we had never been apart. When I had to make a decision to give up my apartment, she invited me to come to live with her until I decided what my next steps would be. I jumped at the chance to spend time with her.

During this year at Aunt Diane's home, I decided to focus on a degree in social work with the hopes of becoming a child and family therapist to abused and neglected children. I also left my job at Meijer. I subsequently spent nine months of the year employed as a childcare worker at the Saginaw County Child Receiving Home as my introduction to social work and as my way of giving back to a place that provided me with so much support and comfort over the years. I originally intended to attend Saginaw Valley State University in order to complete my Bachelor of Arts in Social Work. However, Aunt Diane encouraged me to try life outside of Saginaw via going off to college. While completing my studies at Delta College, I applied to and was accepted into the Michigan State University undergraduate School of Social Work with her encouragement.

I'll never forget the joy of receiving that acceptance letter from the Michigan State University School of Social Work. It superseded the exhilaration I experienced once I walked across the stage at Delta with my Associate in Arts Degree in hand. To cap the year off, before I left for Michigan State, Aunt Diane surprised me by coordinating a surprise interview with the Saginaw News. It felt surreal to know that my story up to that time and my career goals would be reflected in the newspaper of the town that I experienced so much pain within. I still can't describe the feeling I had when I had the actual newspaper article in hand.

It didn't take long for me to locate an apartment within a nice residential section of East Lansing, MI. Words cannot convey the enthusiasm with which I packed, and otherwise prepared myself for relocation. I had great support from Aunt Diane and family members in making a smooth transition. My August 1997 moving day was indescribable. I had never been so excited in my life! During the drive to East Lansing, I was able to review my life through to that time with a sense of great pride, gratitude, and relief pertaining to what I had overcome in order to arrive at that day of transition.

At the age of twenty-one, I felt that I was on my way. The world was full of infinite impossibilities, and I was just beginning to hit my stride. I had found my voice and began charting my pathway. I was Michigan State University bound. My heart felt free, my mind was clear, and I felt very assured of and confident within my purposes and my capacity to fulfill it.

Erica Lynn White

Epilogue

ON JUNE 1, 2019, I stood before the Pastors of New Covenant Christian Center, Dr.'s Ron and Georgette Frierson, other esteemed panelists, and participants as a guest panelist for the churches annual New Covenant Christian Center's Women to Women Ministry Health and Wellness Seminar. This moment was monumental for me as it represents my personal and professional life coming full circle. I presented from multiple perspectives of having experienced trauma, having been a participant in emotional health services, and from the perspective of being a Therapist and Owner of my own private practice (IMPACCTT Enterprises, P.L.L.C of Saginaw, Michigan).

I shared important information and resources regarding mental health, and a portion of my life experiences (childhood and adult years twenty-seven through thirty). The objective was to highlight the importance of my Christian faith and previous use of therapy resources during my own healing journey to those in attendance. I experienced so much joy and freedom in being able to use my clinical knowledge, and life story as a tool to educate, encourage, inform, and inspire.

On that morning, I realized that in this season of my life, with God as my life partner, there is more power in my voice and courage within my person than I ever realized. It feels so great to be *ME*! At the young age of forty-three, I'm able to look back through time at the me that I *USED* to be with the eyes of compassion, love, understanding, and pride. I feel compassion for the things that I suffered. I have understanding for the past behaviors I engaged in—and bad choices that I made when my soul was wounded. I have self-love, pride, and an indomitable spirit. I have love for that past child and the beautiful woman I am today. I was very honest and worked very hard at submitting my pain to God. I consistently worked very hard at conquering who I *USED* to be, and I utilized God given resources in order that my pain could be transformed to healing.

I thank each and every one of you who have taken the step towards investing or re-investing in yourself by reading this book. The sharing of my life story will continue within my next book, Volume II: *The Woman That I AM: Life Beyond Childhood.* I invite you to further share my journey detailing how I healed from trauma, and the processes involved in the healthy development of the woman that I am today.

As I previously stated in the intro, I hope that this story inspires you towards a pathway of healing. Commit to letting the past pass, and do not bypass putting the hard work in to do so. Putting in the hard work may entail 1) fully committing to your faith walk; 2) becoming involved in emotional health therapy; 3) taking medication (if medically necessary, and recommended/ monitored by a doctor or psychiatrist on either a short or long term basis) to help manage your emotions; 4) exercise; 5) developing hobbies, and/or 6) identifying/ disconnecting from unhealthy relationships. Do whatever you have to do for you (that is healthy) even if it is different than what you or the people you are surrounded with have ever done.

Resources

If you suspect child abuse or neglect, please contact your local Child Protective Services Unit. Your state's Child Abuse and Neglect Reporting Number can be located via the **Child Welfare Information Gateway; click this link: childwelfare.gov.**

Michigan's toll-free Child and Abuse and Neglect Reporting hotline number is 1 (855) 444-3911. Children should be seen, heard, and believed as our most vulnerable members of society.

If you are an adult who has experienced unresolved childhood abuse or neglect, please seek supports via an experienced trauma informed therapist.

If you are an adult who has experienced or who is experiencing domestic violence, please seek supports via your local authorities (courts and police), local domestic violence shelters, and a trauma informed therapist. **The National Domestic Violence Hotline number is 1-800-799-7233.** You are not alone.

About the Author

Erica Lynn White, LMSW

Erica resides in Saginaw, MI. She is a proud mother of two beautiful daughters, Dariyah and Rain. Erica engages in motivational speaking and community education. Erica has experience with a broad range of topics pertaining to emotional health improvement. Visit her website at https://impacctt.com for more information and details. She is available for speaking engagements at local and surrounding organizations, schools, and churches. To request Erica's speaking services for your event, contact her @ 989-443-4682, or ericawhite@impacctt.com.

Erica White, LMSW is the Owner/ Clinical Therapist at IMPACCTT Enterprises, PLLC located at 3444 Davenport

Avenue in Saginaw, Michigan (IMPACCTT.com). IMPACCTT is the acronym for Innovative Mentoring Passionate Advocacy and Creative Community Based Treatment Techniques. The vision for IMPACCTT Enterprises, PLLC was birthed out of Erica's experiences within the Saginaw County Foster Care System wherein she experienced some of the best and worst aspects of the system of care.

Erica overcame the past via addressing and overcoming the past. Erica knows that extreme hurt can transform into healing. Erica had to overcome trauma, grief, and loss, so she's been there. Erica provides creative outpatient individual and family therapy services for children, teens, and adults to include senior citizens with abuse, neglect, grief, and/ or loss histories. Erica uses therapeutic tools such as cognitive behavioral therapy, mindfulness therapy, trauma-focused therapy, and psychoeducation. Play therapy is available for children. Telehealth (video) sessions are also available when clinically advisable. Weekend sessions are offered.

Erica believes that although an individual may be or may have been affected by past or present life challenges, those experiences need not define the client or serve as either a complete or a permanent barrier(s) to progress or productivity in a person's life. Erica believes in the power of therapy and faith towards assisting clients with tapping into and nurturing their strengths, accepting themselves

(flaws and all), and learning how to heal, learn from, and ultimately use life challenges/life experiences as catalysts for growth and/ or change when possible. The willingness to work on one's self is one of the most challenging, but ultimately the most rewarding act of bravery, kindness, and love that one can offer to themselves and their loved ones.

Erica believes that the key to successful resolution of emotional health challenges is the courageous use/application of spiritual truths and therapeutic and/ or psychiatric resources towards acknowledging challenges, discovering their root causes, and then applying healthy life skills and skills learned in therapy towards regaining personal power. The therapeutic relationship is a powerful, safe, and nonjudgmental partnership wherein the therapist lends their skills in service as a support towards assisting their clients towards arriving at the client's definition of "their best selves".

Erica holds a degree as a Licensed Masters Clinical Social Worker with a focus in practice with Children, Teens, and Families. She was trained as a Public Child Welfare Fellow within the art of creative therapy and forensic assessment within the University of Michigan Family Assessment Clinic (1999/2000). Erica also hold a Juris Doctor of Law Degree from the Thomas M. Cooley Law School (2008). She has over ten years of clinical experience as a Social Worker. She also has eighteen months of past experience within Legal Services of Eastern Michigan and Legal Services of South-Central Michigan.

Erica Lynn White

Acknowledgements

To God my Father, my Lord and Savior, Jesus Christ, and the Holy Spirit. This is a power packed trifecta whom I cannot live without. All of my dreams are rooted in my faith in Christ, and my capacity to carry them out occur by God's grace and through the power of the Holy Spirit; Posthumously to My Grandfather Joe Swilley and Aunt Diane Staples for cheering me on, pointing me towards a healing path, and loving me unconditionally when I didn't know how to love myself; My brother, Dante Swilley for always believing in me, rooting me on, and encouraging me throughout all of the seasons of my life. You are my first and my forever best friend. Thanks for trusting me to write this portion of the story.

To Dwan Bryant, a wonderful woman of God who celebrated the success of this book when it was still in its infancy. Thank you for being you; My Writing Coach, Minister Jeri Darby. Thank you for lending your full self to this project. You encouraged and provoked me to dig deeper in order to write with excellence and at my highest level. Thank you for the anointing you possess in inspiring writers to strive for and achieve their creative capacity. Your services are invaluable, and you are simply the best at what you do.

Co- Pastor and First Lady Georgette Frierson and Minister Marcia Michelle Reeves, two dynamic women who gave me my first platform to verbalize a portion of my story and testimony. Thank you both for trusting God's voice and believing in me. I don't have words for what that meant to me. To everyone referenced, and to everyone who invests in my ministry by reading this book, I love you and pray God's absolute BEST for you and your loved ones.

Coming Soon!

The Woman that I *AM*

Life Beyond Childhood
Sexual & Physical Trauma
Volume II

Erica Lynn White, LMSW

Erica will share further significant details from her life,
discuss the impact of previous childhood and adult
trauma upon adult relationship choices and outcomes,
and discuss her healing journey (the processes and
supports involved in the healthy development of the
woman that she is today).

Erica Lynn White

www.ingramcontent.com/pod-product-compliance
Lightning Source LLC
Chambersburg PA
CBHW070322290526
45791CB00003B/1212